W9-AHB-172

FACES OF MEDITATION

Swami Rama
Pir Vilayat Khan
Sr. Francis Borgia Rothluebber
Rabbi Joseph Gelberman
Munishree Chitrabhanu
Usharbudh Arya, Ph.D.

Edited by S.N. Agnihotri and Justin O'Brien

HIMALAYAN INTERNATIONAL INSTITUTE
Honesdale, Pennsylvania

ISBN 0-89389-044-8
Copyright 1978

HIMALAYAN INTERNATIONAL INSTITUTE
Honesdale, Pennsylvania 18431

All Rights Reserved

Preface

Meditation is no longer a strange thing to the West. Actually, meditation has always played an important role in Western culture from Hellenic times through the Middle Ages into our technological society. Its influence upon society has been uneven. Yet where a religious or philosophic tradition has appreciated a state of tranquility, emotional integration and self-control in its followers, some form of meditation has been preserved and encouraged.

There is a general axiom that states: methods differ but the goal is the same. People meditate for various reasons. For some, it is an act of worship, to be included in their private and public acts of prayer. Others pursue it in order to satisfy their quest for self-knowledge, while still others use meditation for its therapeutic value. Whatever the purpose that inspires one to meditate, there are common benefits that accrue to the practitioners of all genuine paths of meditation.

In this volumn, some of the enrichment of meditation is shared by practitioners of five different traditions. Each author spoke at the first International Conference on Yoga and Meditation sponsored by the Himalayan International Institute. Those attending received their words with such approval and enthusiasm that we felt compelled to share them with a wider audience.

S. N. Agnihotri, Ph.D.
Justin O'Brien, Ph.D.

Contents

Relevance of Meditation to Modern Science

Swami Rama

Before I speak to you, I would like to recite three verses from the most ancient scriptures of wisdom, the Upanishads. They are universal. You can enjoy them:

> *Om.*
> *Asato ma sadgamaya.*
> *Tamaso ma jyotirgamaya.*
> *Mrityorma amritam gamaya.*
> *Om Shantih, shantih, shantih.*

> Lead me from the unreal to the Real.
> Lead me from darkness to Light.
> Lead me from mortality to Immortality, my Lord.
> Peace, peace, peace.

So often these days spiritual teachers and religionists belittle science, but I don't agree with them. If you do not have electricity for light fixtures, I don't think anyone is going to come and listen to you. You cannot travel without car, train or airplane from one place to another. Science has a place in our lives, and by condemning it we do not teach religion. Physical sciences are necessary for modern man and modern man cannot conduct his duties without the help of the physical sciences. As religious, philosophical and mystic truths are important for the unfoldment of human life, so the scientific attainments are a necessary means for our external life.

There are two diverse sciences. One is called physical science and the other is called the science of consciousness. The physical sciences discover the laws of the gross aspects of the universe, while the science of meditation discovers the internal states of human life.

A man is a citizen of two worlds—the world within and the world outside. He has to know the general laws of science to conduct his duties in the external world, and at the same time it is important for him to know the means of unfolding his inner being. Inner and external worlds are mingled. In fact, they are inseparable. He who has known the ways and methods of understanding his internal states reflects his inner wisdom through his mind, action, and speech, and conducts his duties efficiently in the external world.

When I lived in the caves of the Himalayas,

there was confusion in my mind regarding the modern scientific way of living. I used to separate the scientific way of life from the religious way of thinking. The day came when I discovered that religious truths need a scientific systemization, and science needs a religious philosophy. All the great scriptures talk about the same truth, yet the followers remain unsatisfied and ignorant. Believing in the great scriptures, and having faith in them does not give me direct experience and satisfaction. Without having direct experience, the study of the scriptures is not satisfying.

I always tell my students, "You worry too much about enlightenment. Start treading the path of inner light." When you tread the inner path you will not need a scientific instrument like a telescope. The telescope is of no use for seeing within. Seeing within is an entirely different art and it needs no external instrument. Of course, it takes some time for one to become an insider, because our daily living teaches us to be outsiders all of the time. In our society today a prosperous man is known by his progress in achieving things and possessing them. But, if he does not possess peace of mind and contentment, all of his possessions are useless. We need to have inner tranquility and equilibrium to live peacefully in the world. I have met many rulers and rich men, but I did not find them in peace, and did not find any happiness in their lives. Happiness is a symptom of inner peace, and peace comes through having a tranquil mind.

All the meditational techniques described by different scriptures and taught by different masters are very brief techniques. By merely knowing the techniques one cannot understand the entire philosophy which lies behind them. Meditation consists of a right technique, a sound philosophy, a strong desire to experience the reality, and regular practice. The Desert Fathers and the sages of the Himalayas believed in meditation. Meditation is necessary for all human beings.

Indian children learn meditation by following their parents. An Indian woman meditates in her actions the whole day. Outside every village in India there is a well where the women go to fetch water. Each woman puts a vessel of water on her head, she moves, talks, and dances, but the vessel doesn't fall down because she remains conscious of the vessel no matter what she does. If we learn to do the things that we have to do, and remain aware of the center of reality within us, that is called meditation in action.

The great Buddhist meditative tradition teaches meditation systematically. The Christian Bible says, "Be still and know that I am God." The technique that helps you in being still is called meditation and the revelation therein is called God within.

There is no conflict in the practice of meditation. The school of meditation is free from religious fanaticism, symbols, ideas, fancies and fantasies. Anyone and everyone can meditate.

Meditation should be accepted as an essential science for individual and group therapy. It helps me in becoming a creative genius in the world and in having a tranquil mind all the time. Scientists start and stop with relaxation, while the science of meditation goes deeper than that. When the deeper methods of relaxation are experienced, one comes to know that all relaxation methods will gradually lead one to self-control, though the meditator is not conscious of this fact. Too much relaxation without conscious control can become harmful. If one allows his muscles to remain relaxed for a long time the muscles may lose their natural contraction. Moreover, relaxation based on suggestions is not part of meditation.

During meditation, the muscle life, nervous system, and various functions of the mind are brought to a state of balance and tranquility. That relaxation which gives you conscious control over tension and relaxation is the right method. Relaxation is necessary for meditation, but not the type of relaxation based on suggestions.

Meditation is an inward journey in which one explores his internal states, finally reaching that center of consciousness from where consciousness flows on various degrees and grades. If the method is practiced regularly and systematically, it is not difficult. Preparation for meditation is more important. When a housewife practices meditation she becomes a perfect housewife. All the scientific attainments in the external world, all the comforts of modern life, can become a means if we know that they are means only. Modern man suffers on account of several self-created diseases, such as hypertension, ulcers, migraine headaches, and depression. The cause lies within the mind. And when the mind is trained through meditational practices, meditation becomes an essential therapy in daily life. It prevents many diseases. When the mind and its modifications are controlled through meditation, one can enjoy inner serenity and do his duties properly. Through meditation alone, one can consciously come in touch with his hidden potentials. To become creative and dynamic, meditation is very important.

A man of meditation is never horrified by the problems of life. He is never tossed by the charms, temptations, and attractions. He remains unaffected in all circumstances of life, good or bad. Through meditation, every human being can do tremendous good for humanity. The greatest obstacles in the path of meditation are created by the ego, and one who knows how to surrender the ego receives the higher knowledge.

I'm going to tell you a story which illustrates the ego problem. There was a young man, a fellow traveler, sitting beside me in a train. There was also a very old swami traveling in the same coach. The young man put a question to him, "Sir, have you controlled your anger?" He said, "Yes, it's easy. I've never lost my temper. I have no ego. I have perfect control over my anger." But the young man persisted in asking the same question again and again. He went on asking by saying, "Really? You have no anger or ego? Have you really controlled your mind, action and speech?" The old swami lost his temper and became very angry and said, "Shut up! And if you don't, I'm going to bang your head!"

The hidden personality of everyone comes up during odd situations. Actually, this is a period of self-examination. One can overcome all the odd situations by being aware of the center of consciousness. To maintain this center consciously is meditation. Inner strength is higher than external strength. Those who have inner strength remain undisturbed all the time.

I met a swami who was a realized being. He was speaking on meditation, and one of the students got up from the audience and said, "Sir, if I say that you are a fool will you be disturbed?" The swami said, "No." The student said, "Why?" The swami said, "I do not easily accept suggestions from others; I have learned to remain calm and comfortable."

A man of meditation understands gestures, emotions, thoughts and desires. He is aware at all times on all levels. There is a vast difference between hypnosis and meditation. There is a difference between prayer and meditation too. Hypnosis helps one on a superficial level, meditation is something different; it helps one in facing the reality. It leads one from duality to unity.

Adler, James, Freud, and even Jung knew that although hypnosis is helpful on a certain level, it cannot lead one to a deeper state of consciousness. Meditation is unity in diversity. As long as you see forms and names, you are under the influence of hypnosis. The whole of humanity is hypnotized by external conditions. We don't need more hypnosis. Hypnosis and meditation are two different concepts. In one you need suggestion, and in the other you directly experience the reality. No method of hypnosis can enlighten you. Yes, it can put you into deep sleep. But sleep cannot enlighten anyone. When a fool goes to sleep he wakes up as a fool. But when a fool goes into deep meditation he comes out as an enlightened one.

Often students put this question, "How long will it take for me to learn to meditate?" My answer is, "How long will it take for you to light a dark room?" If you have light, you can dispell the darkness. And how long will it take for you to light it? A second. If you are fully prepared, if you learn not to waste your time but to utilize it for preparation, you can know the deeper levels of your being. All problems will be over if you willfully and consciously spare some time for meditation. A few minutes every day will help you in forming the habit.

When the habit is strengthened, the mind starts flowing toward the grooves created by your habits. For those who have been doing meditation, the hour of meditation is the finest hour of the day. All human beings, in their ignorance, commit mistakes. Meditation makes them aware of their mistakes and gives them freedom from guilt complexes. Meditational methods help you in becoming aware of both good and bad qualities within you.

Another question students ask is about a guide or guru. Modern students have an image of the guru as a supernatural human being—an image which reflects their own ideas. A guru is he who thinks, speaks, and acts according to the dictates of his own conscience. The highest of all gurus in human form is he who practices and is experienced himself and who guides you selflessly on the path of enlightenment.

The scriptures say, "Wake up from the deep sleep of ignorance, prepare yourself, learn to listen to your own conscience, and do not follow the tricks played by your mind." Do not waste time in knowing the different paths, but follow one path with all sincerity and faithfulness.

Meditation in Sufism

Pir Vilayat Khan

I greet you with the greeting of a dervish, *ya azim*, which means, "How beautifully do you manifest the divine glory to me."

I would like to subtitle what I have to say, "The Rishi and the Dervish." Fundamentally, I am sure we all believe in unity rather than uniformity, and so I feel that both the rishi, who is lost in the vastness of the mountain, and the dervish, who sits in the squalid streets of the city, have a contribution to make to our thinking and our feeling and our lives. Therefore, I would like to think of them as complementary rather than in any way antagonistic or mutually exclusive. Now I know that all generalizations induce one to error, and therefore I don't want to make too much of a generalization. But I would say that the way of the rishi in the Himalayas is the way of one who wishes to surround himself with a zone of silence, the nostalgia of the one who seeks to find the cause behind the cause, to go beyond the walks of men and see what it is behind all things that makes them tick. Whereas the dervish, I think, is trying to find meaning in fullness, in life. This may be an exaggerated distinction between the two, since Hinduism is a vast reality and so is Sufism; within each you will find the most various forms of aspiration. But I think there is a fundamental dichotomy in the strivings of sensitive human beings.

One is, as I said, longing to reach beyond what the Sufis call manifestation, which means to be liberated, to be free. Nobody likes to be conditioned by circumstances, and so the kind of meditation that is sought after is *samadhi*, which is a way of awakening from the ordinary consciousness in which most people are entrapped. As a consequence, in *asamprajnata samadhi* for example, which is the highest form of *samadhi*, the experience of the physical plane seems to have fallen out of focus. One experiences that state which is called *nidra yoga*—deep sleep. It is really introducing consciousness into deep sleep. It is a tremendous feat for a human being to maintain the continuity of consciousness in what appears to be sleep from the point of view of those who think they are awake. It is really an awakening for those who realize that most people are in a state of sleep. In fact, we can reverse our whole way of thinking. We generally think about sleep from the vantage point of our so-called awakened condition, which is really a kind of sleep. Few of us remember what it is like to remember our everyday life while we are sleeping. But if we can remember our dreams when we are in our ordinary state of consciousness, then surely when we are asleep we can remember our everyday consciousness. I'm sure that at the moment we realize we have awakened from our earthly condition, we also realize how very much we have let ourselves be caught up in our trips and all our strivings.

We couldn't see the wood for the trees. Has it ever happened to you, for example, to have come to regret that whatever you wished for ten years ago actually happened? We do let ourselves get caught up in things and then later on we awaken from them. In fact, the whole of life could be considered as an awakening. I believe there are two dimensions to awakening. There is the awakening in which you have to withdraw your consciousness from the physical plane so that you're able to see behind the scenes, as it were, the cause behind the cause. And beyond the cause, even, as you would find in Vedanta. Among the Sufis one can speak of being awake in the middle of everyday life. Curiously enough, the best definition of what the Sufis are striving for is to be found in the words of Shankaracharya. It's the story of a person who was walking in the jungle at night and thought he saw a snake. The following morning he saw it and realized that it was a rope. If he were to walk by the same spot the next night, he would realize that even though it really does look like a snake, it is really a rope. This is being awake in the midst of everyday life. You see somebody caught up in his trips, and you see the aspect of yourself which is tempted to get enmeshed in this whole situation in which most people find themselves, but somehow you are able to see through it. This is a second type of awakening.

Most forms of meditation strive towards awakening. Perhaps you could say that there are three main aspirations of a human being. One is liberation, another is awakening, and the third is realization. Maybe there is another one, and that is illumination.

I am sure that many people feel that liberation means being free from the conditioning of outer circumstances, so that one doesn't have to return for a further reincarnation.

But it seems to me that the real liberation is liberation from the self. This means that one is totally free. For example, people may insult you and it doesn't affect you. You meet with a tremendous defeat and it doesn't worry you. Even if you experience a great victory it doesn't move you particularly. This is being free internally.

This is a saying of the great Sufi, Farid ud-Din Attar, who says, "Renounce the world, renounce your self, and then renounce renunciation." I would like to add, renounce renunciation out of love. Dare you renounce renunciation out of love? Sometimes I wonder if it isn't the height of selfishness to want to be liberated. Isn't it better to bind oneself out of love in order to free others, rather than trying to free oneself? We have to consider our motives in what is called spirituality. We also have to consider the different methods which are used in meditation.

What exactly are the various forms meditation assumes in Sufism? The most typical Sufi is the dervish; actually, in Iran they say dar-veesh. This is a very rare type of human being whom you hardly ever run across these days. Perhaps if you were lucky going through the lanes in the desert you might come across a dervish walking into his village. But woe upon you if you follow him into the village. What defines the dervish is that he has allowed his mind to be totally blown by facing the meaningfulness of things. You see, we protect ourselves from the deep meaningfulness of things by our philosophical concepts, by our mental constructions. It takes a lot of courage to face meaningfulness, and the fact is that the computer which is the mind is not capable of facing the power of truth. Consequently, the Sufi will always say, "Oh, I am so overwhelmed, I am so shattered." In fact, one is never so strong as when one is broken, and one is never so happy as when one has no reason to be happy. So you can say that the dervish is someone whose mind has been blown, to use a modern American term, and whose heart has been broken. The dervish is madly in love with the only being whom anybody ever does love, who is God. I know the word God has become old fashioned now, so I tend to say the one you love. And that says everything. As Ibn Arabi, one of the greatest Sufis says, "He is the one whom every lover loves in every beloved."

Somehow, in the depths of the human soul there is a tremendous nostalgia for what the Sufis call "the very being of whom one is the projection on the earth plane." It is not just a mental need to know the principle of one's being, as Aristotle says, but a deep need in the soul of man to see outside himself that which he really is inside. In fact, as you know, we can only unfold ourselves by discovering ourselves in another ourself; in fact, by discovering ourselves in the universe. I think that meditation is a process of self-discovery. We must think of it as creative, and not just a trip; it must do something to you, otherwise it's just a trip. Meditation is part of the meaningfulness of life.

So, as I say, the dervish is someone who has a broken heart. His heart has not been broken because of a love affair that was rather desperate and perhaps fateful, but his heart is broken because he has become sensitive to the sufferings of all beings. I know these are easy words to say, and I don't like to philosophize and sermonize people. But I can only say that if you enter into deep communion with people, you have a feeling for the *tonus*, for the nature of the emotion of people. You'll find that there are those who are very sensitive to what is happening in the world, and there are others who say, "Well, I don't care, it doesn't affect me." This sensitivity makes the heart of a being the heart of the universe. Once my father, Hazrat Inayat Khan, was giving a lecture and suddenly he had to stop and leave. Somebody asked, "What happened?" He said, "Thousands of people are asking for help; there's been a terrible catastrophe." A few hours later we read in the papers that there had been a great earthquake in Japan; I think it was in 1924.

What I mean to say is that the heart of the dervish becomes so sensitive that he is able to be aware of the suffering of humanity. The consequence is that he develops a tremendous intuition. For example, there is a story of a dervish in Hyderabad who was walking down the street laughing his head off and weeping bitterly at the same time. You might think that is a hysterical state to be in. Actually, when anyone came near him he could tell them all about their lives: why things were the way they were, what could be done to change things, and so on. He knew absolutely everything about everybody. How did he do it? Because he didn't know who he was, where he was going, what he was doing. Therefore, he knew everything about everybody else. That's what I mean by not only having your mind blown, but your heart broken and your soul split. You remember the words of Jesus when he said, "He who loses his life shall find it." Well, I can say that the dervishes are following that precept. If you care, life does that for you, and it gives you a joy that you could never have otherwise. That's why there is this wonderful blend of joy and pain.

Now, you ask, what is the meditation of the Sufi? At first it is like following this nostalgia, looking for that which the rishi is seeking beyond life, in life itself. It is the same thing; it's a matter of seeing beyond the appearance. First one is in a state of absolute bewilderment when one discovers the marvel of all created things. The Suifs say you discover the footprints of the beloved. It's as if you were looking for a bear and you saw the pug marks of the bear in the snow. Well, you haven't seen the bear, but you're getting closer. If you are in love, you can discover the beauty of the one you love; if you're not, you can't; you only see the surface.

There is a very deep emotion behind the meditation of the Sufi, which contrasts with what might be called the way of sobriety. Here one may compare Sufism and Buddhism, because as you know Buddha leads one from joy into peace. This is what one does if one seeks a way apart from the world and beyond the world. Of course, in Buddhism too there is a return into the world; there's no doubt about that. But if you have a sense of the meaningfulness of life on earth, then your seeking will be there. I know that we would like to see behind the scenes, because that's where the offices of the architects of the universe are; we would like to see the blueprints, and we think if we saw them we would know what it is all about.

But in fact there is more in a house than in the blueprints. Why do you want to look for the blueprints when you can live in the house? That's why the Sufi Nifari says, "Why do you seek for God up there? He is here." There's a real sense of meaningfulness which cannot be accounted for by the cause. The cause is like the law. If you drop a coin in the slot you get the candy bar. If you drop a stone from a tower, it takes so long to fall. You did something ten years ago, and all of a sudden you have to suffer for it. That's the law.

Some things can be accounted for by karma, but there are many things in our lives which cannot be accounted for by karma. There isn't just law; there's also love. There is a spontaneity in what the Sufis call the programming—well, perhaps that's my interpretation of the term; they say *ma'ana*, the divine intention. And you see, God is free from his laws. So while there is law, there is also freedom within it. What happens to you is sometimes a way of making you realize something. It is not because of something that you did before; it's because of the programming, because you are being guided. You are placed before a test. It is much more to the point to see the meaning of our lives than to understand the cause of our lives. This is the reason why in Sufism so much emphasis is placed on the meaningfulness of what is hidden behind the surface of things.

As a consequence the Sufis always say, "Physical reality or existence is a veil on the face of the beloved." They always use the word beloved because they are centered on love rather than understanding;   you could say there's an understanding of the heart. If you come across a group of dervishes together, you will find them saying the most wonderful things and being delighted in their togetherness. One will say, "Oh, how I would like to see the face of God!" The other says, "But God does not have a face. He is beyond form." The next one says, "The forms of the universe are the forms of his face." And the other says, "Yes, but his countenance is hidden behind his face." And then the next one says, "I am the divine face. Oh, take away my being so that I may come in contact with his real being. I am standing in the way of my experience of God." You have this need of the Sufi to annihilate himself, or rather to let himself be annihilated so that he may come closer to the beloved. This is absolutely typical of love in its extreme form. This is the first step.

Of course I'm talking about meditation in everyday life. One doesn't have to withdraw from the world and sit in a cell. Life is the most wonderful opportunity because we meditate. Here we might compare Sufi meditation to the Buddhist practice of *satipatthana*. There's a great similarity, because *satipatthana* is also meditation in action.

The next step in meditation according to the Sufis is contemplation. The word contemplation is used instead of meditation. In the *Yoga Sutras* of Patanjali you start with *dharana*, which is just concentration. You experience yourself as being what you think you are; at least, you think you are what you think you are. The object seems to be other than yourself, outside yourself. This is *dharana*, concentration, and you try to limit the number of things you are concentrating on so that you have a deeper grasp of them. In the next stage, *dhyana*, you experience yourself as the object; so much so, that you feel what you would look like to a rose.   You are looking at the rose, and you experience what the rose sees of you.   It is as though you have transferred your center into the rose.   Now this is very typical of Sufi contemplation.   There is a loss of the frontiers of the self because one has been so deeply annihilated. As a consequence one experiences oneself as the self of all beings, which is exactly what you find in the *Isa Upanishad*, for example.   It is a wonderful feeling actually: being freed from the tyranny of the ego.   And of course it gives you a completely different vision of things, a very wonderful vision because life is very limited when seen from the vantage point of the individual.   Imagine that you are seeing from the vantage point of all creatures at the same time. It becomes so wonderfully rich.

The next stage in the meditation of the Sufis is to see the attributes, which are the first layer behind the appearance of things, the physical reality.   For example, somebody comes into the room and he is very peaceful.   Many people would say, "Isn't it wonderful to meet this peaceful person."   But the Sufi would say, "Isn't it wonderful to see divine peace manifesting through this person."   In other words, his consciousness is geared to the attributes rather than the physical expression.   So behind all

things he sees their meaningfulness; he reads
the meaningfulness of things. He feels that all
creation is a means whereby the one he loves is
able to manifest himself, and he is delighted to
be able to see this manifestation of the one he
loves before his own eyes. One could say that
the sight of the elephant hides the majesty
behind him. If you can just focus on, zoom in
on the majesty and forget the elephant, then the
message comes through to you. That's why
Farid ud-Din Attar says, "Every leaf reveals its
secret to the one who is seeking the mystery
behind creation." This stage is the discovery of
those subtle forms of reality hidden behind
physical things. The Hindus call it *panmantra*,
which means the subtle reality.

Then the Sufi undergoes a kind of crisis.
The object has been transformed in the sense
that he sees the reality behind it, but what
about the subject, me? The one who is conscious: what about consciousness? If you think
you are the one who sees, then of course you
limit your experience to your sense of yourself
as an individual consciousness. You know that
one of the three principles of Buddhism is *anatta*,
which means "no entity." So there's no such
thing as individual consciousness. That's the
real *maya*. *Maya* doesn't mean this is not a

a table, it means that things are not the way they seem. I am not at all what I think I am. When I say that, I mean not only my personality, whatever that is, but my consciousness as well.

So the Sufi passes through a crisis where he feels that he is imposing a limitation on the consciousness of God which is passing through him. The first attitude of the Sufi is "I am the eyes through which God sees." In other words, there is a consciousness of a greater consciousness working and manifesting through one's consciousness.

Those of you who are interested in the parapsychological research which is being done in our time will know the book *Psychic Discoveries Behind the Iron Curtain.* You will remember that they started experiments in intuition with twins, or with a mother and child, just because they have something in common. Let's say there is a kind of group consciousness behind individual consciousness. And if this is true of twins or a mother and child, then it is true of all people. The whole thing is to reach planetary consciousness beyond individual consciousness. While Jung spoke of a collective unconscious, I think we can speak of a collective unconsciousness which is the awareness of our awareness. *Satipatthana* consists of watching yourself walk and you think, "Isn't it extraordinary that I can make this lump of flesh move?" Now you can watch your mind ticking, and you think, "Well, that's the way minds are made. Why do I think I'm thinking?" Watch yourself thinking. You can actually withdraw the center of your consciousness from the body consciousness and from the mind and watch yourself. Who watches whom? There are several layers of being, and the higher you get the more cosmic they are, and the less individual. The higher they are the more impersonal they are, and the lower, the more personal. Then you reach further and watch your emotions, watch yourself happen, watch yourself reacting. Then you are able to see yourself as the object, as the other side; instead of assuming that you're the person who is acting, you see yourself objectively.

Then at a certain stage you watch your consciousness. That's getting really interesting, because then you see yourself as the universal consciousness watching the personal consciousness which is just a part of itself. Now this brings us very close to the meaning of Sufism, because we said "You are the eyes through which God sees." You are the individual consciousness and the overall consciousness is God seeing through your eyes. According to *sati-patthana* you actually identify yourself with the cosmic consciousness and center yourself there. Of course there's a difference between being centered in your private, personal conscious-ness, and experiencing a consciousness as passing through you; or then centering yourself in cosmic consciousness and watching personal consciousness from that vantage point.

This latter, which is found in Buddhism, is also to be found in Sufism. I would say it is really the highest level, the highest step men-tioned by Al Hallaj, who was a great Sufi master who was crucified because he said, *"Ana'l Haqq."* This means, "That in me which says 'I' is God." Al Hallaj says that as long as you are conscious of your individual self you can only think of yourself as an instrument of the divine glance, but once you are annihilated you are the divine glance. It's a kind of awakening; some-thing happens to people at a certain moment when they awake and suddenly realize that they are the divine glance. In other words, the person you were looking for in the universe is deeper in yourself than yourself. As Islam says, God is closer to you than your jugular vein. This is a way of speaking about the intimacy of the divine being in yourself.

This is a kind of crisis in consciousness for a Sufi. Imagine that it happens to you. One doesn't know how to cope with the new vantage point because one is so used to thinking in terms of one's individual consciousness. This is the reason I say the mind of the Sufi has been blown. He can't use his mind any more because it is meant for certain limited operations. It's like the Euclidian geometry you learned at school. Then we hear from Einstein and others that it's only valid in certain limited applications; when it comes to sidereal distances, then it doesn't work anymore. So we speak about non-Euclidian geometry. In the same way, our little minds function in certain ways which are all right for everyday operations, but when it comes to really seeing things in their fullness then the mind is not capable of dealing with it.

Curiously enough, a kind of universal mind takes over. It is very difficult to explain this because we always think of ourselves in terms of individual self. But the same thing is to be found in yoga, in *turiya*; what Gaudapada says is that *Atman* takes over. Up to that point you were operating from the center of your individual consciousness; from that point onwards the *Atman* takes over. The total consciousness takes over from your individual consciousness.   At that point you not only experience yourself as the being of all beings, but also as the consciousness behind all things.

Now there is a struggle, because there is always a vestige, a residue of personal consciousness which comes back again. So there is an oscillation in the consciousness of the Sufi between the divine consciousness and the human personal consciousness.   This dichotomy is expressed as a kind of *cri de coeur*, a kind of agony on the part of Al Hallaj when he says, "Oh God, take away this 'I am' from between thou and me."   That's the reason why the fundamental practice of the Sufis is the *zikr: La ilaha illa'llah hu*, there is no God but God. One level it means there are no idols and so on. Esoterically it means that there is only one being. The real *maya* is multiplicity. It seems to us that there are a lot of beings, but in fact they are like the cells of one being. We lose ourselves in multiplicity and forget the unity.

In a sense we can say that Islam affirms the unity, and that is the strength of Islam. Sufism, having its roots in Islam (though I believe that it originated far before Islam in the time of the Iranian Magi, the Zoroastrian Mazdean tradition), adopts this practice which consists in affirming the divine being. This is the most powerful thing that can happen to a human being; it's the reason for the tremendous power of the dervish.

Most people are afraid if they come in contact with a dervish because he looks right into your eyes and sees right into your soul. The first dervish I saw was in Pakistan. I was visiting Gulaam Muhammad, who was the Prime Minister. His son was the head of the Pakistan airline. I asked if he could take me to see a dervish in the streets of Karachi, and he said, "Well, you take this street there and you turn left and . . . " So I said, "Well, can't you take me there?" "Oh, no, no, no. I don't want to get anywhere near him." "Why?" "The last time he cursed me and I was so scared that when I crossed the road I broke my leg. As a matter of fact, if I hadn't broken my leg I would have taken the first flight of Pakistan airlines which crashed." So I said, "Well, if cursing you did that much good, why don't you let yourself be cursed again?" It's the power of truth. Of course the Sufi has blown his mind and blown his soul and so on, but the consequence is that his being becomes very, very powerful. But the power of his being is not personal power; we must be very careful of personal power. Unfortunately we are living in a time when people with personal power have more success than anybody else and people like to follow like sheep. People like to follow a great big ego because it gives them self-confidence. One wonders, where is the ideal?

The ideal is to be found among those who have totally annihilated themselves in the divine consciousness. When the divine consciousness comes through, it is very powerful. This also applies to oneself. Meditation is a process of self-discovery. So you watch yourself from the vantage point of your eternal being. Our personality is something like a plant that has unfolded out of a seed. Our eternal being is that seed. The seed may sprout in different ways through different lives, but in a sense there is less in the plant than in the seed. Supposing the seed doesn't have enough sunshine, or enough water? Then it will not unfold as well as if it had rain and so on. So the personalities of some people give you a false impression of their real being. The thing about the Sufi is that he sees the eternal being of a person behind his personal being. And, in fact, that is the only way to see people. Otherwise you judge people by what they appear to be, which is not what they are . . . *maya*. And most of us are judges of other people, when all that we know is the surface, the appearance of people. That's why Martin Buber spoke of the "I-Thou" relationship and the "I-It" relationship. He spoke about entering into the being of a person, and you can never judge a person when you feel a part of his being.

This means being able to see the reality beyond transformation, beyond becoming, beyond process, beyond change. That's the seed. For example, if you try to remember what happened to you two years ago and then four years ago, right back into the past when you were in your mother's womb, you will suddenly come across your eternal being and become conscious of who you really are. There are many layers built upon that, like your environment and your education; all those things have masked your real being. And also there is less in the personality than in the seed. But there is also more, curiously enough. The personality has taken by osmosis something of the personalities of other beings, because every being is a part of your being. We're continually drawing beings into ourselves. We start speaking like the beings we love. There is an osmosis between beings. This is what is happening on the earth plane, this is the plus of life on earth. These seeds which were on the causal plane, well, they had to come together, to be able to conjoin so that some new reality could be formed. Something is gained by the creation and that's the reason one shouldn't simply return to the state in which one was before one became. That's the reason why we should see where this is all going. The meaning of the new age is understanding the programming, what it's all about.

What is gained by that? You can say, the plant is transient, it's going to die, so what remains of it? The perfume. Millions of roses can fade away but the perfume is still there. And that's the meaning of resurrection. Resurrection is very important to the Sufis because it is of no use just letting yourself be annihilated. The whole thing about annihilation is to survive, but transfigured. It's the message of Christ, there's no doubt about it.

Al Hallaj was crucified because he said, "*Ana'l Haqq.*" In Arabic there is a contrast between *haqq* and *halk*. *Haqq* is like *purusha*, it's that which is not transient, that which is always there. And *halk* is creation. So what Al Hallaj said is, "That in me which says 'I' (that is, my personal consciousness) belongs to *purusha*, belongs to that which can never change." But there is part of me which is involved in the process of becoming. The verdict on Al Hallaj was not only that he should be crucified, but that his body should be burned. For a Muslim this is a terrible condemnation. I don't know if such a thing was thought of before, but for the Jews and the Muslims the body is going to resurrect, and so if you destroy the body it cannot resurrect. When Al Hallaj heard this news, he said, "Oh, how is it possible that having wished for the formation of this body, Thou wish that it should be crucified and burned?" And then he said, "And go off as smoke in the four winds." And then he said, "As an incense promise of my resurrection." All of a sudden he understood that in fact the body had to die so that it might resurrect.

So the sense of resurrection is very strong in the meditations of the Sufis. They said, "Die before death, and resurrect now." You don't wait for later. And that means, become the perfume of your being. Let go of that which is passing, because if you hang unto it you'll die with it. Let it go. You do survive, but you survive as a perfume.

I spoke of being the eyes with which God sees, and then of being the divine glance. Al Hallaj says about this, "How do you think you can add something to the vision of God? Do you think that you, by being the eyes of God, can do something that he wasn't able to do? And then he said, "In a minute he can suddenly, absolutely shatter your understanding." That, then, is the purpose of Sufism.

I'd like to end by speaking of what I feel is the end purpose of all end purposes, which is the awakening of humanity. Our lives only make sense in terms of all of us together. No person is important in himself. So many people following the path of spirituality are seeking awakening for themselves. But isn't it much more important to understand that something is happening to humanity in our time, which is the awakening of the consciousness of humanity to the divinity in man.

Now I must try to explain this. Divinity in man—it sounds shocking to some people because they think God is up there and man is a very important being. Hazrat Inayat Khan, my father, said one day, "Christ could very well call himself the Son of God. Because the one who is conscious of his inheritance can claim the inheritance from his father." If you are conscious of the divine perfection in you, then you become the divine perfection. What is happening to people in our time is an awakening of the consciousness of humanity to the divinity in man, not up there beyond our reach. It's like the discovery of what is happening on the earth, the fact that there's a transformation even in the state of God. In fact God is being born in each one of us.

Q: Can you speak of the relation between Sufism and Hasidism?

A: Very close. We belong to the same tradition. The Hasidism, the Jewish mystics, their relationship to Sufism is so close that sometimes when I read the books of Martin Buber I think, well, this is absolute Sufism. And I suppose that it is because of the religious background, let's say the monotheistic religion, but there's more to it than that. Because of course the two cultures have been very close together in the desert and there has been an osmosis between the two. And, well, sometimes we quarrel, but in our hearts we belong to the same family.

Now we have as a matter of fact a Rabbi who is also a Sheikh in the Sufi Order, Zalman Schachter. He is glad to be able to show the unity.

Q: Can you say something about music?

A: The Sufis of the sect to which I belong, the Chishtis of Ajmer, use sound and particularly music in meditation.   As a matter of fact, Sufis attune themselves just as one tunes a violin or any instrument by the use of sound. My father was a musician who founded the Sufi Order in the West.   He said one day, "You should not be surprised if the religion of the future should be music."   I wish I could express myself in music rather than in language.

Meditation in Christianity

Sister Francis Borgia Rothleubber

It is difficult to know what "Meditation in Christianity" should encompass. All I know is that meditation, meditative prayer, is a very real part of our living. I know also that we have come to some new awarenesses about it. It seems to me that the meaningful thing that I could do is to share with you the journey that we are on. We are about a search. That search is best described in a sentence by T. S. Eliot: "We are returning to the place we started from and know it for the first time." We are on a journey that is both a return and a leaving, that is moving to a future that we really do not understand, but that we welcome.

Meditative prayer has been an integral part from the very beginning, an integral part of the Christian experience. We know that it was integrally part of the life of Jesus: the movement to the desert, the movement to the mountains, or out to the ship on the water, was a very real part of his living and breathing into his life. But, in a sense, we are concerned not only with those special times, those meditative, reflective times. We are concerned with the whole way of living, an approach to living. In fact, early in the Christian experience it was simply called "The Way." A way of living in relationship with the Source of Life, a universalized Jesus, who energizes and makes possible a rooting in reality that alone we could never, never know.

This experience is the living of a parable. A parable is an answer that does not answer. It is always an answer that is both a challenge and an invitation. It is the paradox of living a truth in reverent tension, discovering a truth in reverent tension. It is losing one's life at the same time one finds it. An emphasis on the Way, the Christian Way, that would be just losing one's life, would lead to a passive pathology, an illness. Finding one's life leads to an illness, a violent aggressiveness. We need the paradox of the losing and the finding the Paschal Mystery, the journey that is both dying and rising. This is the paradox to which we are invited.

This paradox, lived by the early Christian community and recorded in the Gospels, has been interpreted in a variety of ways across the ages. It would be an intriguing study sometime just to parallel the early Ignatius, who spoke of that water that kept drawing him to come to the Father, and the later Ignatius, whose whole approach to reflective prayer was carefully organized. Think of the differences of a Teresa of Avila, a Therese of Liseux, think of Julianna of Norwich, of Francis of Assisi, of Catherine of Sienna, Alfonsus Ligouri—almost such divergent approaches to reflective prayer in the Christian experience that it is difficult to get them encompassed into one approach. They are like facets, different ways this Gospel experience is interpreted in a given culture by a given personality.

It is difficult to talk about meditation. I think of Frederick Franck's account of opening a seminar with a very careful explanation of the Zen of Seeing/Drawing, and then deciding the only way was to go and do it. Go outside, sit down in front of that leaf. Look at it so quietly that it takes over and you can draw it without looking at the paper. That leaf has entered your reality. It is that entering reality, learning to breathe into your own life, that no one can lead you. There are ways to help you start, but you must find, each of us must find that way of breathing that fits us, that within which we savor life, we come more alive. It is something of this experience that I would like to share with you, both reflectively and as we can, in a kind of living into it together, making it possible for you to enter something of such an experience.

Perhaps before we begin the experience, it would be helpful for you to understand that religious women in the United States, Roman Catholic, Anglican, Lutheran, religious women, Christian women, are about an exodus, responding to a call to move into a different way of living, a freedom and a searching that until now we have not known. Our foundresses began, generally, in the 19th century, began in Europe, for the most part, or if not, transferred to the United States the European, 19th century approach to religious life for women. Our congregations were generally organized to bring together a group of women who were interested in the immigrant who had come to the United States, women who wished to teach, women who wished to serve in health care or social service, women who were asked to build into their lives the cloistered, the contemplative cloistered approach to silence, of certain restrictions to travel, of controlled scheduling of time with provision for work and prayer. The question before us following Vatican II became: how can we minister to life so that we truly anoint it? How do we anoint life within us and around us? Healing. How do we take that experience of Jesus, that is ongoing today, the Spirit being poured into us, anointing us, that we can direct outward to free, to heal? To arrive at this possibility we have taken beginning steps in a new journey that we are finding more and more life-giving. They are old steps, but they are newly discovered. We find that we are learning that our meditative prayer is less a separation from life, as it was thought to be formerly, a stepping out of life to get a perspective on it, and much more a dialoguing with our experiences, a dialoguing with life.

We are finding that as women in this century, we need to approach the Christian message in a whole new seeing. In many ways we have been masculinized, many of us, men and women, have been masculinized by our experience in Western Christianity. The call for us to incarnate those values that have been set aside in the process of masculinization, the value of interiority, the value of compassion, the value of communion. These values are suspect, generally, in our society, are looked upon as weak in contrast to the successful dominating approach of being first, having the most, being "in control." Today we think of our reflective praying less as the prayerful saying so many words, and more a growing into our life, being more and more honest about who we are and what fits well within us, and what is leading us to greater freedom and greater energy.

We are learning that in a masculinized society the concept of a woman's body carries negative overtones that women have interiorized and that must be rethought. We are rediscovering the sacredness of our bodies. We are learning to breathe more deeply, learning to take joy in our body, in the good sense of the body smiling. We are learning ways of becoming still, quieting, finding ways of centering. As I work with young women today I discover that they find even five quiet minutes very long, almost intolerable. We are learning the way sound, sustained rhythmical sound, can help us to center. For most of us the symbolic, the meaningful word, is quieting and awakening.

I would invite you then to breathe deeply for just a moment, just to taste the experience which many of you go to rapidly and quickly. I am going to begin a simple chant based on a phrase that is very present to me this season: "the tree." The tree was such a significant part of our reflection at the early Easter season, the tree planted near living water, the tree rooted down into living water. As we breathe more and more deeply, call out into our whole being that light. Let it flow out into us. Personally and as a whole group together here we are tree. We are sharing this life, almost tangibly here. Let that life come up in us to energize us, to free us. And as the melody gets familiar to you, come along, come with it, harmonize with it.

Tree drawing light through its roots.

Tree drawing light through its roots.

Tree drawing light through its roots.

Into the quiet we read the word of scripture. The passage that is with me today is from Isaiah, 50:4, 5.

The Lord Yahweh has given me a disciple's tongue. That I may know how to sustain the weary, he provides me with speech. Morning after morning he wakes me to hear, to listen like a disciple. The Lord Yahweh has opened my ear.

Everything depends on how we read the silence around us and within us. Everything depends on how we read the silence. We are, Paul writes, a people seeking His Face, groping, moving, knowing that in Him we live and move and have our being. We are learning that that which is yearning is not separated from that which is God, that Loving Presence who energizes us, energizes our human life that comes to fullness in a faith relationship. We are learning to close the gap, the separation of natural and supernatural, human and divine.

As we breathe and reflect we are entering more fully into the Source of Life that burns like a river of fire in each of us. We are learning that to come into touch with that river of fire, the closest way to do so is to come into our own reality. Openness to life, opening our hands, learning to open our whole being, letting our past come before us, owning and accepting our feelings, knowing how to hold into the Light that which is our fear, that which is blocking us, that which is disappointing us, that which is oppressing us, that which is giving us joy, that which is opening us to other people, a new friendship—whatever the feelings are, to let them come into the Light. Within that very experience sleeps the call that morning after morning we need to hear. Yesterday's word is not today's word and we have not yet tomorrow's word. It is morning after morning we listen for the new word of this reality within which we live. The more we are in touch with the Source of Energy, the more freely we can walk with risk, respond to the exodus call, creating and being energized in ways we had not thought

Drinking more and more of that living water that we have been promised, and that is there for our drinking.

We are learning to listen to the word that is in other's lives also. Learning that the same Source of Energy that is within each of us is shared. There is one energy, so that we need not be in competition with other people. We need not seek to objectify, put people into boxes or make them fit into roles. That same Life is calling out life in them and the more the people with whom we live are energized the more we are energized. We set up currents of support and currents of vitality, generative of all kinds of new ways of anointing life. The recent almost creative explosions that are beginning to happen among religious women are simply the beginnings of this kind of initiative, creative energizing. Nothing is alien to our humanness, no joys, no sufferings are other than our own.

Moving and flowing into life and letting life move in and transform. Discovering the very special presence of the Lord among the sick and the oppressed, a very special Word, and a special call. The approach, the dichotomy that we have been wrestling with between prayer and justice is unnatural. Nothing wholesome and

lasting can occur that is not grounded and rooted in interiority, in a non-violence within oneself.   At the same time, attentiveness and alert-
ness move us toward making sound changes that
can reshape human society.

We are on a journey. I believe a very good
journey. I know it to be good in my own life
and I see it good in the lives of other people.
I am learning that it is not so much a question
of the East and the West coming together as it
is a question of what is human. What is fully
human? Whenever we can discover what brings
us to greater fullness of life, that is where our
journey takes us. It is today that we are to be
on that journey.

Let me conclude with the prose-poem
story from the Talmud. Our Christian tradition
flows in and out so closely with the Jewish
tradition, and this will be so very much what I
have been trying to say.

In the Talmud, the following history was
told: About 250 A.D., the Rabbi Joshua Ben
Levi met the prophet Elias. He asked him,
"When will the Messiah finally come?" The
prophet answered, "Go and ask Him yourself."
"But where can I find Him?" "He is sitting
among the poor and the sick, and binding up
wounds." Rabbi Joshua Ben Levi then went to

Rome, and there he found the Messiah, sitting at the gate, just as the prophet had described. He went to Him and said, "Peace be with you my Lord and Master."   And He answered, "Peace be with you also, son of Levi." "When will my Lord finally come to redeem us?" The answer was, "Today."   Rabbi Joshua Ben Levi returned to the prophet and said to him bitterly, "The Messiah tricked me.   He said He would come today. But He is still not here." To that the prophet replied, "So long as you don't know what 'today' means, He cannot come at all."

Q: How do we dispel the dogma of some religious conventions which deny that the Raja Yoga meditation tradition is valid in Christianity?

A: Well, how do we dispel the dogma? I don't know. I just believe that the more we pursue the Gospel, the early Christian experience, read it in the Jewish practices, the more we begin to understand that this meditative prayer, reflection, the whole tuning of the body, breathing all is very naturally part of it. Again, I think we come to the question of what is life-giving for the person, not what are the dogmas. What is life-giving?   And the guide in that experience, refined and shared in community, is life.

The other question: does yoga include Jesus in its teachings? Can Christians include yoga in their teachings? I think this is the same question.

Jewish Mysticism

Rabbi Joseph Gelberman

I come from a mystical Hasidic tradition, and in my tradition you are very conscious of the fact that the world has been created in harmony, and the object and the purpose of every human being is to keep it in harmony. And unless we are in harmony with the day, the day will pass us by. This is the reason for all the frustrations, anxieties, and tragedies.

So every morning every child—the minute he begins to learn how to talk, or even murmur—learns a prayer, a prayer of affirmation. Some of you here who have a Jewish background—and haven't denied it yet—may remember. The prayer is called *modeh ani*. It's a simple prayer of thanksgiving that the soul has been returned unto me. And with this affirmation I'm a part of the harmony today.

I think to be in harmony with tonight, I would like to ask you to join me in an affirmation, a sentence that is taken from the psalms, saying, "This day is a day of light and a day of joy, a day of perfect realization." *Yom zeh*, affirmation in the Hebrew. I know you all know Sanskrit; it's about time you learned Hebrew!

I'll chant a phrase, just like we do it in yoga. I too have been practicing yoga now for over twelve years and next year I'll have my yoga *Bar Mitzvah*. Then repeat the phrase after me, and then we'll hum it together. "This day is a day of light and joy, a day of peace and harmony."

As a preparation for mystical studies, we keep in mind again the unity of the whole being. And in order to purify the body—not to cleanse the body—the mystic goes to what is called a *mikvah*. That's a special ritual bath, for the purification of the body. I will bathe the fingers because they represent the whole body. This is where it all begins and all ends. Plus, the ten fingers are symbolic of the ten *sephiroth*, the ten attributes of God in kabbalah. If you are with me, you should feel the coolness of the water all over the body. And thus we prepare the body for the study of kabbalah.

Next we have to prepare the mind. The mind is symbolic of light, we are told in the Bible. So we need a light. You know the phrase when two people have a discussion, or a so-called dialogue, and one tries to convince the other, and finally the other says, "Oh yes, I can see it now." And we understand, we comprehend. A light goes on. This is part of the eternal light in each one of us. So we light candles at our sessions. We light two, like every Jewish home has for the holidays, and here in mysticism and kabbalah the two candles are symbolic of the two inclinations in each one of us.

There is a constant civil war going on to do or not to do, to go or not to go, to be or not to be. Traditional religion would suggest that you fight the evil, so that the good may succeed. But mysticism says that is a waste of energy. Concentrate on the light, on the good, and therefore the object is to bring the so-called good and the evil, symbolic of the light, together. Again, harmonize it, until you no longer know which is which.

All you know is that there is great light. A torch of light. And this is a very important symbolic lesson in kabbalah: two have become one. Remember, it's still two. And in terms of the soul, the *b'shamah*, we usually at our sessions sing the melody. Consider yourself, therefore, prepared for the study of kabbalah, called

Jewish mysticism.

Actually, there is very little difference between mysticism, Jewish or Christian, except for the fact that Jewish mysticism has a lot to do with the Jewish people, with the Jewish experience, with the Jewish dream, with the Jewish hope. But the idea of a mystical interpretation of life, for good, for joy, for redemption of the inner soul, of the inner self, must be the same.

As it is true as far as all religions are concerned, the question is not to which religion one was born or one belongs, the question is which way are they going. Are they going towards the top of the mountain, which symbolically stands for God? Then we shall meet, perhaps surprised: "You are also here?" Usually, when we fight each other and hate each other because of religious difference, it is because we are not going anywhere. We are standing still. As a matter of fact, since there is no such thing as standing still, we are going down into the basement, into the darkness. We don't see anything. The same thing is true with Jewish mysticism.

The Hebrew word for mysticism is kabbalah. Kabbalah simply means "to receive"; to receive that which is implied in the Torah.

The Torah is our Hebrew Bible—each letter, each word, and the space between the letters. According to the mystics, when the Torah was given on Mount Sinai, the kabbalistic interpretation was also given simultaneously. But many of us didn't listen because we were not prepared.

So kabbalah means when we reach the point of listening, of being ready, then we can receive that which is there, which was there all the time. Kabbalah also means to be like a television set. It's an antenna. You pick up that which is in the air. Nothing has been lost. God spoke on Mount Sinai about three thousand years ago, "I am the Lord Thy God," and that voice can be heard today. This is the difference between the saints and the ones who are not saints yet.

Buber said this very beautifully. He said, "There's no difference between holiness and un-holiness, or saints or sinners. The difference is in time. Some of us are not there yet. We haven't reached it." But nobody's a sinner by definition—unless he is unhappy. The Baal Shemtov was the founder of the Hasidic movement and lived in the eighteenth century. He would be what you would call the Jewish St. Francis of Assisi. He was that kind of a man. He used to say that the greatest sin is having a

melancholy attitude. And he preached all over
the world the concept of *simchah*, the concept
of joy—which has nothing to do with happiness.
You can be very unhappy, and very joyous. Do
you understand? But there is a difference,
because happiness has to do with outer things,
while joy has to do with inner things. If I know
who I am, and if I know that I am connected
with a spiritual umbilical cord to my heavenly
Father and that cord can never be cut off, then
by definition I have every reason to be joyful.
And the other things are just annoyances.

So, when people ask me, "How do you
feel?" I usually tell them, whether I'm at home
or in the hospital or wherever, I tell them
"I'm not always happy, but I'm always joyous."
Tonight I am both. I am joyous and I am
happy!

So, I should like to explain just one
Hebrew letter kabbalistically. Those of you
who know, know we have twenty-two Hebrew
letters. The twenty-first is called *shin*.

Now, some people ask me what this
emblem, this mystical emblem, is all about.
The *shin* stands for many things, but it especially stands for *shechinah-shadday-shalom*. They
all mean God's mystical name. It's made up of
two words. The One who said, "Enough." On

the sixth day, when He finally created man at twilight, he said to himself, "Enough. From now on I shall do nothing by myself, but you and I together will finish the creation." The Bible finishes the story of creation with the words *asher barah Elohim la-asoth*: "Which God has created to finish." The implication is very clear. He did not finish the creation; it's entirely up to us to finish it.

People come to me and ask me all kinds of questions: "Where is God?" "Why doesn't God do anything?" I think in this generation we finally have found the answer. In olden times we used to live in apartments, and if something went wrong, we would call the landlord. We would immediately curse the landlord, and do all kinds of things saying, "Give us hot water, cold water, fix this, fix that!" So he was the land lord. So it is with God the Lord. If something goes wrong, we knock at the land-lord's door using prayers and all kinds of things—like a telephone to call to God.

But now God is telling us if you are really listening to the answer, "I am not your landlord. I am a member of the co-op and we're doing it together." It's no use crying out. Those kinds of prayers are completely worthless. Nobody is listening. So *shadday* means the one who created, who said, "Enough" and gave man the beautiful, the highest title we can ever achieve, called *shutaf Elohim*: "a partner with God in creation."

So this is the word *emeth*. On the top you will find the three Hebrew letters, the *alef,* the *mem*, the *tav*: the first, the middle and the last. Put together they stand for *emeth*, truth. God stands for truth. He has many, many names, almost as many as they have in the Indian culture. But *emeth* is the most important name: truth.

Underneath is the four-letter word ,in kabbalah known as the *tatragramaton*. Only the high priests knew how to pronounce this name. And they pronounced it only once a year on Yom Kippur, on the Holy of Holy Days. The minute the people heard it, they got the message, and the benefits of it, and immediately forgot it. And since the destruction of the holy temple and the entire priesthood, nobody knows how to pronounce it. The Christians read it *Yaweh*. When we come to read it in the Bible we simply say *Adonay*. But every mystic ever since Rabbi Simon Ben Yochay—who according to tradition was the originator and author of the book called the *Zohar*, the kabbalah book—ever since then, every kabbalist is preoccupied with finding the pronunciation of these four letter words, because finding it, you would know how to redeem the world.

Now we have come to some idea. Not exactly, but through numerology we have an idea what the four letters mean. Let me put down here two circles symbolic of the upper and the lower world. So this is the upper and the lower two circles, and it's combined with seven balls called the seven rungs of meditation. The Hebrew word for meditation is *kavanah*.

Each letter stands for a concept, and therefore it gives you the method of how to meditate. I'll mention only the English because it will take too much time otherwise. The "k" in *kavanah* stands for *kitov*: that all is well. It has to be, if God created the world. If God is good and love, then it must be good and love. The second letter is *ahavah*: love. To express love every day, every moment in our lives. The next letter stands for *vi-dui*: to confess our shortcomings, to be mature enough to say, "I've made a mistake." The next one stands for *ne-oth*: meaning "to let go." And the phrase is, "Let God take over after I have done everything humanly possible." The next one stands for *amunah*: faith, even blind faith. And the

seventh one stands for *hitlahavoth*: the ecstasy, the fervor, the excitement. Now these are
the seven rungs that keep the two wheels together.

Now if you take the numerology of these
four letters, the first letter, the *yod*, is ten (every
letter has a numerical value); the second one,
hey, is five, the third, *van*, is six, and the fourth,
hey is five. How much is it altogether? Twenty-
six, two and six, which added together come to
(26 = 2 + 6 = 8). So we have some idea by
saying the four letter word, the number eight, to
create the number eight by combining the upper
and the lower word. Thus we can bathe in the
presence of God.

Then you will find here also the word
chay which means life. Here I want to take
you back to the Bible. Remember the story of
the Garden of Eden, which was a wedding present from God the Father to Adam and Eve.
He said, "It's all yours. You don't even have
neighbors to worry about. No government, no
nothing. It's all yours, everything. Except,"
he said, "you see those two trees in the corner,
called the Tree of Life and the Tree of Knowledge? I don't want you to touch them or to
eat from them." I think God made a mistake
here. If he would have kept quiet, it never

would have occurred to them to touch those trees. But, as you remember, they did. They ate, if you remember, of the Tree of Knowledge. Out of this came the big to-do about original sin in the Catholic Church, and even in the orthodox Jewish Church; that we're condemned already from the beginning, and only through grace can we redeem ourselves. I'm suggesting to you the exact opposite.

The original sin was not that they ate of the Tree of Knowledge, but rather that they did not also eat of the Tree of Life. Because look what happened: they ate of the Tree of Knowledge and they became really knowledgeable, especially as far as technology is concerned. We can push a button either in Washington or Moscow and the entire world will go up in smoke. But we have not yet learned how to live with each other, either nation with nation, or neighbor with neighbor, or husband with wife.

What the *shin* means here is this kabbalistic emblem—which also contains a mantra inside—that we must also taste of the Tree of Life. And tasting of the Tree of Life is exactly what we're doing here, but we have to do it more often. I hope all of you, when you go back to your communities, will become missionaries in that sense. Not to tell people what to do—don't ever do that. But rather be like this light. If you put out all the electric lights, do you think this candle will go around saying, "Hey look at me, I'm a candle!" Do you think it would do that? Nothing is as disturbing to me—and I'm sure it is to you—when I meet people, especially the ones who come back from India, and the first thing they tell me is how enlightened they are, how saintly they are. And you know what I do? I collect money and send them back.

Because if you really are a light, you don't have to tell anyone. So don't tell anyone what to do. But be a light unto your people, unto your neighbors, unto your community, so that you can be a light unto the world. And be yoga, which is unity, and *shalom*, which is peace.

Q: Do you have to know Hebrew to study the kabbalah?

A: Yes. I would say at least know the Hebrew alphabet, the twenty-two letters. And I would suggest that, if you take the twenty-two letters as twenty-two individuals, you can fall in love with them. Then you don't have to know the rest. But it will help.

Q: Can you say something about the Ein Sof?

A: The *Ein Sof* is the kabbalistic name for God. It simply means "the circle," the One who has no beginning and no end.   You will remember the greatest contribution of a human being is his thumb.   The monkey has all the others.   But when we got this thumb, then we said, "Now we can work.   We can take a tool in our hands, and really become co-workers with God."   Kabbalistically, because of the thumb we can make the sign of the *Ein Sof*.   And the three remaining fingers are the *shin*.   So when I give the benediction, for example, you know the old way that the priest would give it was like this.   And I use this sign as a reminder of God's name and the relationship that I am in this partnership.   We are not doing so well these years, but still the partnership goes on.

Q: Are there some writings in the kabbalah which are not being revealed?

A: I don't go along with that idea.   I know that that is a rumor.   Why should God do that?   Why would He give us something and then say He doesn't want us to know it?   But we must be ready.   Before Einstein came, we never knew anything about relativity. Anything that was there for the consumption of His children. And get as much as you can. That which you don't understand, put it away for next year, and grow. I once asked my father, when I was only about eleven years old, "Why should I read the Bible again, the same stories, the same as last year's. Nothing has changed." And my father was a very wise man, and he said, "That's true. But haven't you changed since last year?"

So the Bible will talk to you in a different way each year, each time. And this is why the Bible is a best seller still. And you can burn it, as they did in many countries, but it's still a best seller because it speaks to every individual— if you are listening. The Bible is like a woman. You have to understand her as much as you can, but most of all you have to love her; and when you love her, by golly, she'll give you anything, everything, and do anything, everything for you.

Q: How do you integrate yoga with your Jewishness?

A: How would I integrate? Like I integrated tonight. I had chicken, and some vegetables, and they were all a part of the dinner. I personally don't see any problem. As I said earlier, let me make a little picture here. If this is the top of the mountain, and this is where God is—and this is just symbolic—and here we all are down below the mountain, and what did you mention? Yoga? One is on the yoga path, and one is Jewish. If we are both going towards God, where is there a conflict? I don't see any conflict at all. Not mentioning the fact—there was a famous kabbalist called Abulelfia, of the 12th or 13th century, who did what we call today yogic meditation, sitting on the floor, having a candle in front of him. Every Jew even today does as I have done long before I knew yoga. On Thursday night, in preparation for the Sabbath, I would sit on the floor for an hour and do meditation. The question always is: what is the aim?

For example, some people came from California and some from New York. And here we are. If we all go up the mountain, we will all be with God, and there is no problem at all.

Meditation in Jainism

Munishree Chitrabhanu

This is a beautiful time, and a unique occasion to meet souls who are on the path to find their own light and their own self. When we meet such people who are sincerely seeking, from without to within, it becomes a moment of communication and a moment of bliss, a time of unity and union.

In all the religions you will see that the seekers have striven to see the inner light. Whether it is Hinduism, Buddhism, Jainism, Christianity, Judaism, Taoism, or any other religion, each started from the quest to see the higher self and transcend the lower self. According to the geographical conditions, the environment, and the needs of the seekers, each religion has given some insights to them.

I would like to discuss the ways of meditation from the Jain point of view and give a little background of Jainism and explain how to enter into meditation. Also, we will consider what we want to receive from meditation.

Jainism comes from the word *jina* which means "he or she who has conquered his or her inner enemies." Not outside enemies, but inner enemies. All outside enemies are the result of inner enemies. Instead of wasting time conquering outside enemies, the wise people use their time conquering inner enemies. When you conquer your inner enemies you rule the world without any army, without any weapon. The whole world is with you because your weapons are compassion and love.

Mahavira was the last prophet, teacher, and master in the line of twenty-four tirthankaras of Jainism. A tirthahankara is a great sage or seer, one who builds bridges among men. Mahavira and Buddha were contemporaries, Mahavira being twelve years older. Both were princes and both worked in the same area which is known as Magadha in the north of India. Mahavira was a *jina*, he conquered himself. For twelve and one-half years he observed silence. He did not teach during that time because as long as he had not experienced the supreme realization, he was not eager to teach. It is not easy to have control over the desire to voice your opinions; for that we need the practice of silence.

So Mahavira became *jina*. And those who are eager to follow the path of conquering their inner enemies are known as Jaina. Jaina is not any religion, any sect, or any kind of fold. It is a way of living, thinking, and practice. Any person who follows non-violence, who has relativity in thinking, and who knows the invisible vibrations of the karmas, is Jain. Mahatma Gandhi, the Father of India and a Hindu by birth, followed the message of non-violence and brought this insight into the political movement. He once wrote, "though I was not born as a Jain, I am more than a Jain." There is no baptism, no ceremony, no ritual. By your practice and your life you are a Jain.

The whole emphasis of this philosophy is not on any outside ritual, but it is an inside investigation, awareness, transformation. And to bring about transformation requires transmutation. Inside everything changes. That is why today we are going to examine a few insights of meditation. It is a vast subject, and it takes serious and sincere, consistent and constant awareness to go into meditation. It cannot happen instantly. Real meditation cannot be "instant meditation." Yes, after long practice, in an instant you go into meditation. That can happen, but the person has some previous background, some former experience.

For myself, when I entered this path, for five years I practiced silence. I wanted to know the secret of words, the mystery of life, and what is beyond death. Is there real death? When you observe silence, in the beginning you feel uncomfortable, because you have the habit of voicing your opinions, speaking, and making noise, but when you observe silence for a long time you are not ready to break it when the time comes. The peace is so deep in you that you enjoy being silent. Your eyes are open, your ears are open, you are open to the universe. And you are listening to everything, and the noiseless sound.

Silence plays a great role in the path of meditation. At the same time we need inner awareness. Jainism is a path, not a circle; it is moving in a particular direction. That direction is not out, it is in. It is not without, it is within. It is not going anywhere. It is finding yourself in being.

This is the first idea of Jainism. In this search there is no boundary between East and West. The boundaries are of the mind, not of souls. We see human life everywhere, pulsating with eagerness, and having a deep quest in their center. All the souls are equal. If you only see the outer garb you will see that some have white skin, some have red skin, some have black skin. These are all outside appearances, but inside the flame is the same. This is the real essence of Jainism.

Today, we are really fortunate. I am fortunate to meet you, and you are in a way fortunate to hear the message which was permeating the Indian air two-thousand and five-hundred years ago. Now the same message is here. We are experiencing and enjoying it here. America is taking the spiritual lead. It has taken the lead to go to the moon. It is going to take the lead to go into the inside of life.

Now, I come to the inside, to meditation. What is meditation in Jain thinking? Meditation starts with this idea: turn off for awhile your outer activity in order to enter the complimentary, receptive mood of your soul. Because you are always active, you are busy living outside. You are making yourself empty, and you are not fulfilling yourself inside. Without the inner touch your words become empty, your language becomes meaningless, and your talk becomes only a kind of chatter.

Whatever activity you do, you don't really do it on your own initiative, rather, you follow the herd. Because many people are acting a certain way, you do it too. The time comes when a person becomes mechanical in movement; he or she moves but does not know why he or she is doing such a thing, why she or he is speaking certain words. In order to receive, to create the mood of reception, you turn off all this activity.

What do you do then? First you sit for awhile. You take an asana. It is called *kayotsarga*, which means that you forget awhile the body tension and attention. You allow the body to relax in its own way, like a piece of sponge, so that the tension which you have accumulated begins slowly dropping down. *Kaya* means the body, and *utsarga* means to drop. Drop your body. Why? Because as long as there is tension in the body, you won't be able to experience the flow of life.

Do you know how much tension you have? Even as you prepare to meet a person, you are building tension in your body, in your mind, in your brain cells. How to greet? How to meet? How to speak? What to say? In this way, in school, in colleges, in our studies, in our society, in our people—everywhere there is tension. This tension is built in now. Even if you sit for meditation, your body is not quiet. It is jerking. Even though people sit quietly, they go on biting their nails. They make many gestures because there is no quietness. The first step is to drop your body, allow it to live in its own state. When you have done *kayot-sarga*, you can turn to the mind and the breath.

When your breath is under tension, you take shallow breaths. But when you allow the body to flow, the breath goes deep, and you are taking proper oxygen. Your body, when it is filled with fresh, deep oxygen, is animated. The cells are not dead. They are not stagnant. There is no inertia. There is freshness in your body, so you need fresh breath. That is why meditation generally was observed on the top of the mountain, in the forest, near the river, on the shore, in the natural environment. As you take in fresh air, your mind is also blossoming. You are opening, and you feel the freshness of your mind.

In this way, breathing is done, and then if the mind disturbs, you use the word *virum*. *Virum* means to engage your mind. For a long time the mind has been rushing among so many activities, and now it does not know what to do. The five senses are demanding from the mind, therefore it is engaged in many directions.

Now you locate your mind in one place. And that is why we use the word *virum*. It is our mantra. When you breathe in, you use *vi*, and when you breathe out you use *rum*. *Virum* is a Sanskrit word which means "brave." Be brave. Be brave enough to accept the real nature of yourself. It may seem a little contradictory. You may ask, "To accept the nature of yourself you have to be brave?" Yes! To enjoy your blissfulness, to know your inner thoughts, and to be in a relaxed mood, you need bravery, because the mind is loaded with worry, anxiety, fear and many negativities.

As soon as something beautiful happens, we are afraid. We are afraid to embrace happiness. Three days ago one sister came and she told me, "For six days I have been feeling joy. Now I don't know what terrible thing may happen to me." I said, "Why?" She answered, "For six days I am so happy, so blissful. When it lasts for six days, I worry something is going to happen. I don't know what, but I feel it." I told her, "This is your mental tendency."

The mind is not ready to enjoy blissfulness, the *chit* and *sat* and *ananda*. These three qualities are in us, but we don't believe that. We have doubt. We believe only for awhile, on the word level. It will be a great day for you when you believe that "this is my nature, to be happy, blissful, full of knowledge, and immortal.

I am *sat, chit, anand.*" *Sat* means immortal.
Chit means consciousness. *Anand* means bliss.
Friends, this is what is hidden in the body, this
is what we have forgotten.

So we are doubting these three things, as
though they belonged to certain blessed and
higher souls, such as Christ. We say, "Oh,
Christ was the Son of God; Mahavira was
fortunate because he was born in that time.
Buddha was lucky he was enlightened. But
me—don't think of me. How am I to enjoy
that?" We don't have faith that this is our
birthright, our real quality.

Now when you use the mantra, use *vi*
while you are taking in breath, and *rum* when
you are exhaling. In this way you are slowly,
slowly engaging your mind. One psychoanalyst
a few days ago came and said, "Why do you
have to use mantra?" I said, "If you have a
monkey, you have to make it quiet. If you
want to make it quiet, you have to give it a
banana." The mind is a monkey! And this
monkey mind runs in all directions. We are
giving it bananas; a mantra is a banana to this
mind.

Soul does not want mantra, because soul
itself is *sat, chit, anand.* Soul does not need any
mantra because it has the quality of reality. The

time comes when we have *dharma sanyasa*. *Dharma sanyasa* means that you leave behind all the rituals and all the mantras, and you go free. That comes when you are free from the shackles of the mind. That you do when you are free from the bondage of *vasana* or desires. Then you need nothing.

As long as the imprints of the *vasana*, the desires, are there, we are bound with the shackles of longing, of infinite kinds of cravings, and so we are always comparing ourselves with somebody. This is the business of mind. To train your mind, you need something, and this I call mantra. It is a banana for our monkey mind. We say, "Eat and sit, and do not disturb me. Let me feel what I am."

Now we use *virum* and in this way we are going inside for the first time. We experience and we feel calm. It is the first time a new experience is felt. When that glimpse comes, you know you have really reached the state of meditation. Then you feel "I am here."

There are three stages as we go inward. In the first stage, your mind is reciting mantra, but at the same time it is bringing many distractions. Then we use the word *kohum*. *Ko* means "who" and *hum* means "I." "Who am I?" You ask yourself this question: "Who am I?"

Meditation starts with this first step. Without knowing yourself, you will not reach yourself. It is our real self we have forgotten.

Slowly, slowly put this mantram to your mind, saying: *kohum*. Then the answer comes: "I am form. I am body. I am he or she." Your name comes. Your emotions come. Passion comes. You say, "No, this is not me. My name was given after I was born. Somebody has given me this name. What was I before then?" There comes the body. Before the body you were there. You entered the body. But who was it that entered the body? You are going deeper now. *Kohum*. Constantly you go on removing the layers. When you remove the layers of an onion the freshness comes out and when you remove the layers of a cabbage the fresher leaves of cabbage come out. The outer leaves are tough and rotten. We also have many layers, friends, and these psychological layers we have mistaken for ourselves. Because of these layers we are day and night depressed, suppressed, prejudiced, angry, irritated, and unhappy. Think of yourself. How are you using your day? Most of the time we are lost in all these layers. We hardly have time to feel our real nature and experience the inner divinity. We use *kohum* in order to investigate our real self, and we go deeper and deeper and deeper.

Three students came to a master. One was a prince, another was the son of the sheriff, a very wealthy man, and the third was a humble seeker. They all sat before the master. The master opened his eyes, and he asked a question: "Who are you?" The prince smiled and answered, "Don't you know me? I am a prince. I am the son of the king here." "Oh, " said the master, "you are a prince? Very glad to see you."

Then he asked another, "Who are you?" The young man replied, "I am the son of the sheriff. This big garden in which you are sitting belongs to my father." The master said, "Oh, I am very glad to see such important people." Then he asked the third stranger, "Who are you?" He answered, "Sir, had I known who I am, I would not have come here. I don't know. That's why I am here."

An individual who knows himself is lost in himself. He is always in ecstasy. He is never bothered. He is enjoying inner feeling. We all have the birthright to enjoy that state of bliss. If we can train ourselves and transcend the mental barriers we can realize it in this life.

This third man said, "I want to know who I am." He went on, "All the environments and all the situations are creating new conditions, putting on new layers; and layer after layer has come over me, so that in many layers my real self is lost."

Then the teacher asked for a little milk. When the man brought it, the teacher took the milk and put a little yogurt culture in it. Then he asked the man to take this milk and put it aside for twelve hours. It became yogurt. Then he asked the man to churn it and the man did and made butter. Then the master said, "Take the butter and put it on a low fire and make ghee (clarified, purified butter)." So the man made ghee, and then the master said, "See, this ghee was hidden in the milk, but if you put your hand in milk, you won't find it there. This is the process. You have to add culture, and then allow it to be calm. Then you have to churn it and to put it on the fire. Then finally the purest substance comes out."

Friends, this is the light; this is the way to see yourself. First, you have to put a real message of the master in your life. Culture means the right knowledge, the right insight. If wrong concepts enter your head, they will cover all your thinking, and once it is covered, you are lost. Right teaching is as important as right food, right air, right living. Do not follow the herd or practice a religion merely because your father did.   You have to be a seeker. Really speaking, life is meant for the truth—to seek and to find it.

Don't be stagnant and don't follow anything blindly.   Faith is not the answer.   It stops your search, and then you do not go further.   Sometimes faith is a barrier.   Awareness keeps you alert, removing all your layers.

So friends, here the teacher told him to first put the right understanding inside, put in the culture.   But don't shake the milk, allow it to be calm.   When you've taken the right understanding inside, then you sit and meditate and see for yourself.   See how it works for you. Each individual is unique, so don't compare yourself with anybody. Mahavira's teaching was essentially this: you are an individual light, you are you.   You cannot be anybody else.   If you compare, you will bring misery and pain to yourself.   You are not like anybody else, because the vibrations of your karmas are different.   Your vibrations are with you, so if you seek yourself and go within yourself, then you will find you.

For that we must take what we hear and practice it inside.   That requires peace, tranquility, calmness.   And that's why you select some calm spot to go to sit and ask and that inside will slowly settle down. You take hot water and put tea in it, and the tea settles as it brings color to the water. In the same way, the truth must settle. There is no need to be in a hurry to go to the world and make everybody religious. No, that is a kind of mania. You must practice first. How can you help anyone unless you grow and feel a change and reveal it through your life?

One of the best things I like about Mahavira is his silence. He observed twelve and one-half years of silence. Only when he realized himself completely did he speak. Those few things he said still have their effects in these days, for you will be glad to know that today there are two and one-half million people who are staunch vegetarians and who don't even eat eggs. These are the Jains in India. Because this message came directly from within it has lasted for 2,500 years. The life of the master, the life of the teacher, becomes a direct experience. It is beyond words. You see the light, and you follow the message.

The second step in meditation is to take this "milk" and be calm so the culture can settle and permeate the milk. The teaching goes inside and permeates your consciousness; the consciousness which was covered and loaded and filled with worry, anxiety, hang-ups, problems from the past, is freed. When you become calm, you take the teaching deeper and deeper, and then a process of churning takes place. That is introspection.

In introspection you watch all of yourself. Let all your past come before you, and go on discarding. Let it go now. You remain in the present; don't go into the past. If the past wants to come, let it come and go before your eyes. It is erasing from the tape. When everything is erased, your tape is clean. You have to erase from your consciousness and past all those hang-ups which are disturbing you, which are coming in your dreams and in your thoughts, causing your anxiety.

You are sitting here, not going into the past. Live in the now, here. Allow the past to go before your eyes. This is mental meditation. It is churning. The time comes when you are clean. The period comes when you feel the flame and that outer covering has gone. It depends on your intensity, your steadiness, your calmness, your introspection.

When the butter is ready you have to put it on the fire. Fire is called *tapa*. In any life some kind of *tapa*, some austerity, penance, or a little suffering is involved. There is no growth without some kind of giving. In *tapa*, you are purifying yourself, as gold is purified in fire. In the same way, our soul is purified by giving. When this cleanliness comes, your soul becomes pure like ghee.

In the same way as that, oh friend, you will know what you are. So the first word for meditation is *kohum* and to erase, we have the second word *naham*, "I am not this." The third word in meditation becomes this: *sohum*. When you become ghee, you know *sohum*. "I am I." You see that the lower self was thinking lower because it was loaded with lower things, but the lower self is in reality the higher self. There is no difference, they are the same. That is called *sohum*. And realizing *sohum*, we reach the state of bliss.

So friends, it is a process of meditation, and traditionally this meditation takes a long time to learn and to explore, but in a nutshell what I have mentioned is these three words which are used by the Jains to investigate and reach the *sohum* state of yourself.

This way in Jainism some steps and techniques are used. You use meditation in order to reach your higher self—that is its purpose. I pray that you will use this way of meditation and raise your lower self to the higher self, and enjoy the state of *sohum*. This is the message and meaning of meditation, and the Jain way of thinking, living, and enjoying.

Superconscious Meditation According to Ancient Scriptures

Usharbudh Arya, Ph.D.

I pray and pay homage to the long line of gurus stretching back to *Hiranya-garbha*, the golden womb of the universe, the first superconscious principle permeating every mind of the entire universe, the golden womb, the holy ghost who is the first, the last, and only teacher, the only guru in the yoga tradition.

I pay homage to the rishis in whose minds, that were linked with the Superconscious, the rivers of wisdom flowed and became the Vedas, the sacred texts. I pay homage to Gaudapada and his disciple Govinda, and his disciple Shankaracharya, and the line of Shankaracharyas reaching down to my own guru.

In my homage I utter the word *namah, namah, namah*. Not mine. In these words whatever is faulty is mine. In these words whatever is faultless, free of blemish, free of pollution comes from a long line of gurus to whom we pay homage. The gurus who saw in their vast, expansive vision the glimpse of *Brahman*, the Expansive One whose expanse cannot be measured in the terms of the solar systems, galaxies and mere billion trillion light years. This entire universe is, as it were, a tiny twiddling toe. In the Being of that Transcendental One who is perceived by the realized yogis as the one transcending all states, all times, all causation; in whose knowledge the *sat, chit* and *ananda* the total existence, the pure consciousness, the divine bliss, that permeates our entire being, also stretch far into the infinite. And in meditation when the waves and the spider webs of the conscious and the subconscious desires and memories and urges drop and are burned in the fire of knowledge, our individual little minds touch, barely touch, the fringes of infinity, they send out a chant and say that entire universe is the dwelling place of God. They say *Om kham Brahma.* This is void. This is null. This is the most expansive.

They sang out and said : *jyotir, jyotir, jyotir; jyotir, jyotir, jyotir.* Light, Light, Light; Light, Light, Light. They drank this *rasa*, this flavorful juice of devotion, and sitting by their sacred fires that burned in their hearts, they recited. They said: *idam madhu, idam madhu, idam madhu.* This is honey, this is honey, this is honey. It is sweet, it is sweet, it is sweet. And when they opened their eyes from that sweet light to the darkness of the multifarious, relative realities of the world they could find nothing as flavorful, they could find nothing as full of honey and mead as that sweet light, that expansive light, which is also the null and the void beyond words, beyond objects. The human imagination cannot go that far. They said, "It flashed like lightening." When that divine mysterious one appeared, the fire "could not burn a little piece of straw." When that mysterious one appeared, the winds "could not toss a little piece of straw." Like a flash of lightening to which I'm called by a "beautiful maiden" within me, of which my inner beautiful golden maiden tells me, "Go, this is *Brahman*." Flashing lightening, "the lightening within you." She said, "This is the Expansive One." And when Nachiketa was offered the entire earth as an empire, when he was given the choice of music and dance and song and bedecked elephants and beautiful maidens for company," she said, "enjoy these things and in the process they will lose their juices, they will lose their flavor. No, Yama, give me that upon arriving where *na cha punar avarttate; na cha punar avarttate:* one does not return, one does not reincarnate."

When Yajnavalkya said to his wife: "Lady, many kings have honored me. Here are a thousand cows with their horns bedecked with gold. I leave them to you and I go, I renounce the world, I walk away, I wander." "Where do you wander to, my husband?" "I wander to that world of *amrita*. I wander to that world of light from where one does not return to this wheel." The wife asks, "Then will I by having all this wealth that was given to you by your royal disciple, will I achieve that *amrita* sitting here?" She said, *"Yenaham namritas yama kimaham tena kuryama:* where with I shall not be made immortal, what shall I do with that? Lead me from unreality to reality, lead me from darkness to light. Lead me from mortality to immortality."

When the soul rises to the heights of purity, one's choice is very clear. Shvetaketu's father said to him: "Son, my son, these bees gather honey from the rose, from the lily, from the marigolds, from the jasmine. While the honey drop is in the jasmine it says, 'I am of the jasmine.' While the honey drop is in the lily it says 'I am of the lily.' So while human beings are in these bodies, you say, 'I am male.' You say, 'I am female.' You say, 'I am tall.

I am short. I am dark. I am fair. I am young. I am old. I am of this nation. I am of another land.' But when the bees are gathered, the honey drops drop into the honeycomb. Thereafter the honey does not know itself whether it is of the lily, or of the jasmine, or of the rose. From that moment on, the honey knows itself to be 'I am honey.'

"This is the truth, this is the subtle essence, this is the reality. When you have realized that reality, you become the pure self, not of this body, neither male nor female, bearing no titles, beyond all conditions. That ever pure, ever wise, ever free, that truth, that reality. *Tat tvam asi.* 'My son, that you are.'" But Shvetaketu did not understand whereof his father spoke. And he said: "Father, will you instruct me further?" And the father said, "Son, these rivers flow from east to west, from north to south, and they all flow to the sea. While they are bound to the two banks, each one says, 'I am the Ganges, I am this river, I am another river.' The water at that time seems to become that river, but when all the rivers have flown to the one common repository of all waters, to the ocean, then they no longer know themselves to be the Ganges, or various other streams and rivers; they know themselves to be one oceanic water. And all drops of water then belong to that one ocean, so while you are in the bondage of ignorance, you do not know that you are not of this body, you are not of that body. You are not of this person, you are not of that person. But that one drop that is within you, though it is at the present moment bound to the banks of your body, you will soon transcend. For the *bodhi* nature, the pure consciousness is your essential self. That is your only self. You flow to one oceanic consciousness. You are then the cosmic reality that alone is truth and life. You are. You are that. As you place a lump of salt in water, it dissolves in the water and cannot be separated, cannot be seen as separate in the water. But my son, you taste that water! Whether you taste it from this corner of the vessel, or from another corner of the vessel, whether you taste it from the top, or from the bottom, it is one saline water. For the salt has permeated every particle of that water. You look for self. You do not find self. But like the salt permeated in the water, you the self have permeated all the three bodies, all the five sheaths, all the seven *chakras,* the centers of consciousness. You have permeated your urges and your emotions. Know thyself. You are that essence. You are that reality.

Tat tvam asi. My son, that you are.

"And as a mighty tree lies hidden in the seed, but in the seed the tree cannot be seen, so in you lies this entire being of your personality." Thus the ancient rishis of the Vedas and of the Upanishads taught those disciples who sat very close. Though they sat a hundred miles or a thousand leagues away, yet they sat very close to their masters, for their minds were in tune. For when you become close to the master there are no more miles, as you bring a piece of iron to a magnet and join it, there are no more two magnets. There is only one.

So down the line of sages, this teaching of the superconscious meditation has descended. It has been handed down in its purest form; the part of Raja Yoga, the royal path, the path of energy, has been transmitted from spiritual father to spiritual son. It is the path of the solar science. The path of the solar science is such that when this sun shines within you all darkness is dispelled, and as I have said earlier, when the darkness is dispelled, it is not as though there was ever any darkness at all. It is as though there never was any darkness. Then no more questions arise, because that place in the mind from where the questions arise, that split, that duality is healed. The mind is healed.

When the mind is healed, the mind is in a state of health. Normalcy.

Normalcy of the mind is defined in the tradition of the superconscious meditation as a state where the superconscious mind has sent forth its rays and has elevated the individual mind, has raised it so that the individual mind forgets. It forgets one word only. There is one word that the individual mind forgets, completely erases from its memory, wipes out, as though there never was that word in the whole universe. When the superconscious mind has taken over the individual mind, one word is forgotten, one word is lost. And that word is "I." And there arises within you an unknown stream of energy that is gathered, controlled, flowing within the banks of the *sushumna*, and you march to those drums that no one has heard, and people take you for a fool. The wise men of the past have said that if you would like to become wise, then become as a fool. Become ignorant of your individual being. Only when the drop has merged itself with the entire depth of the ocean, can it speak up and say, "I am the ocean." Only when the spark knows itself to be a part of the great conflagration, can the spark say, "I am a great fire." Thus you draw yourself, draw yourself inward. As you draw yourself inward, first your longing grows; your longing for truth grows. Is it true? Are these words true? Does it really happen? Is there such a thing as *bodhi*? Is there such a thing as *samadhi*? Is it possible to have absolute resolve? Is it possible to have total enlightenment? Is it possible to be dwelling within a human body five-feet-six and yet within you, you are beyond all galaxies? First these questions arise, and longing for truth grows, and then you belong, and you know the truth. May that truth of the superconsciousness dawn on you not tomorrow, but today, and may you attain the Buddhahood, the enlightenment, and *samadhi* in this very life. May no one be born among your generations who does not know the expansive, eternal, infinite *Brahman*. May God and the long line of gurus bless us all. Om. Peace, peace, peace.

The knot of the heart is loosened. All doubt vanishes. All questions are answered. All karmas are paid off. When that One Beyond has been seen.

It may be possible for you to take a pair of scissors and cut a piece of the empty sky, roll it up as though it were a piece of leather, and go sell it in the marketplace. But it is not possible for the human being to attain the experience of peace without knowledge of self.

As you walk this earth, it is full of pebbles, thorns, that hurt your feet. Come, let us all gather a great amount of leather and cover this earth so our feet are no longer hurt with pebbles and thorns. Take one foot square of leather, cover your own feet, and the entire earth is covered. These are the words from the tradition of superconscious meditation as taught by Swami Rama.

Those who wish to learn how to meditate, how to attain the conscious state of absolute tranquility, of absolute stillness, so that even though you speak, silence remains, you should find your nearest teacher of the system of superconscious meditation and start on the journey. May you have enlightenment in your life. And may all your questions not be answered—may they be resolved.

About the Authors

Swami Rama   Born in 1925, Swami Rama was ordained a monk in his early childhood and was initiated by a great yogi and saint of Bengal. He practiced various aspects of yoga science and philosophy in different monasteries of the Himalayas. He received his higher education in Prayaga and Varanasi. From 1938 he started teaching Hindu and Buddhist scriptures in several monasteries. In the year 1949 he was installed on the Gaddi of Shankaracharya of Karvirpitham, South India, which he renounced in the year 1952. He lived in Germany and Europe for three years studying Western psychology and philosophy. Swami Rama has written several books and founded centers of the Himalayan International Institute in India, Japan, the United States and Europe. He is most well-known for the scientific investigation of the effects of yoga and meditation in conjunction with research facilities such as the Menninger

Foundation. His work has done much to open Western eyes to the value of yoga and meditation.

Pir Vilayat Khan received his schooling and practical experience in classical methods of meditation in European universities. In addition to the more practical uses of meditation, he inspires high idealism and a mystical mood by speaking to the soul and challenging the minds of his students towards cooperation instead of competition. He has established an international interreligious congress, a community in upstate New York, a theater group, a choir and several youth and adult meditation camps in Europe and the United States. Underlying his poetic and idealistic approach, there is a practical approach toward applying meditation in building a world of enlightened people.

Sister Francis Borgia Rothluebber was cited as one of the most significant voices within the American Catholic Church when she received the degree, Doctor of Humane Letters, honoris causa, from Our Lady of the Lake College in San Antonio, Texas. Sister Francis also received her Doctor of Laws, honoris causa, from Cardinal Stritch College in Milwaukee, Wisconsin.

As president of the School Sisters of St. Francis, she consistantly challenges the American religious to respond creatively to their commitment to make the gospel a significant force in contemporary history.   She has been vice-president and president of America's *National Catholic Reporter*, and a leading author on religious life today.

Rabbi Joseph H. Gelberman was born in Hungary where he received his rabbinical and part of his secular education.   He is also a graduate of the City College of New York and Yeshiva University.   For his preparation as a therapist, he interned at the Mental Hygiene Clinic of Cumberland Medical Center, Brooklyn, New York, where he remained on the staff for two years.   Dr. Gelberman is the founder and Rabbi of The Little Synagogue, the Kabbalah Center, the Foundation for Spiritual Living and the Wisdom Academy. He is also editor of *Kabbalah for Today* and president of The New Seminary. He is widely known as "The Listening Rabbi" and is a student of yoga philosophy.

Munishree Chitrabhanu   took the vows of a monk, promising to protect all life, speak the truth and "take with a joyful heart what is given." As a Jain Sadhu, he traveled on foot more than 30,000 miles and for five years spoke to no one except his master. In 1946 he succeeded to leadership of the Jain Community in India and founded the Divine Knowledge Society in Bombay which operates medical relief stations throughout India and strives to improve the status of women. At the invitation of the Harvard Divinity School, Munishree came to the United States in 1971. He is the first Jain master to leave his country. He has lectured widely in America and worked with church groups and organizations. He is the author of twenty-six books and is currently vice-president of the World Fellowship of Religions.

Usharbudh Arya, Ph.D. Born and trained in the Brahminic tradition of India, Dr. Arya has lived and taught in the United States more than twenty years. He received his B.A. from London University, 1965, an M.A. in Sanskrit, 1966 and a Ph.D. in Literature from the University of Utrecht in 1968. He taught Sanskrit and Indian Religion at the University of Minnesota from 1967 to 1973, receiving the Distinguished Teacher Award in 1972. He published a major contribution to Eastern studies entitled *Rituals and Folk Songs of the Hindus of Suryanam* and has also authored *Superconscious Meditation* and *Philosophy of Hatha Yoga*. Dr. Arya is director of the Meditation Center of Minneapolis.

HIMALAYAN INSTITUTE PUBLICATIONS

Living with the Himalayan Masters Spiritual Experiences of Swami Rama	Swami Ajaya (ed)
Yoga and Psychotherapy	Swami Rama, R. Ballentine, M.D. Swami Ajaya
Emotion to Enlightenment	Swami Rama, Swami Ajaya
Freedom from the Bondage of Karma	Swami Rama
Book of Wisdom	Swami Rama
Lectures on Yoga	Swami Rama
Life Here and Hereafter	Swami Rama
Marriage, Parenthood & Enlightenment	Swami Rama
Meditation in Christianity	Swami Rama, et al.
Superconscious Meditation	Pandit U. Arya, Ph.D.
Philosophy of Hatha Yoga	Pandit U. Arya, Ph.D.
Yoga Psychology	Swami Ajaya
Psychology East and West	Swami Ajaya (ed)
Foundations, Eastern & Western Psychology	Swami Ajaya (ed)
Meditational Therapy	Swami Ajaya (ed)
Art and Science of Meditation	L. K. Misra, Ph.D. (ed)
Swami Rama of the Himalayas	L. K. Misra, Ph.D. (ed)
Theory and Practice of Meditation	R. M. Ballentine, M.D. (ed)
Joints and Glands Exercises	R. M. Ballentine, M.D. (ed)
Yoga and Christianity	Justin O'Brien, Ph.D.
Faces of Meditation	S. Agnihotri, Ph.D., J. O'Brien, Ph.D. (ed)
Science Studies Yoga	James Funderburk, Ph.D.
Homeopathic Remedies	D. Anderson, M.D., D. Buegel, M.D. D. Chernin, M.D.
Hatha Yoga Manual I	Samskṛti and Veda
Chants from Eternity	
Spiritual Diary	
Thought for the Day	
The Swami and Sam (for children)	Brandt Dayton
Himalayan Mountain Cookery	Mrs. R. Ballentine, Sr.
The Yoga Way Cookbook	